NATIVE * AMERICAN * CULTURE

CHILD REARING

Leigh Wood

Series Editor
Jordan E. Kerber, Ph.D.

* * *

ROURKE PUBLICATIONS, INC.
Vero Beach, Florida 32964

Printed in the United States of America.

A Blackbirch Graphics book.

Library of Congress Cataloging-in-Publication Data

Wood, Leigh Hope.
Childrearing / by Leigh Wood.
     p. cm. — (Native American culture)
    Includes bibliographical references and index.
    ISBN 0-86625-537-0
    1. Indian children—North America—Juvenile literature. 2. Child rearing—North America—Juvenile literature. 3. Indians of North America—Social life and customs—Juvenile literature. [1. Indians of North America—Social life and customs. 2. Child rearing.] I. Title. II. Series.
E98.C5W66   1994
392'.13'08997—dc20
                                      94-5878
                                         CIP
                                         AC

Contents

Introduction

The words "Native Americans" and "Indians" create strong images for many people. Some may think of fierce warriors with bows and arrows, tomahawks, and rifles who battled the U.S. Cavalry in the days of the Wild West. Others probably imagine a proud and peaceful people who just hunted buffalo and lived in tipis on the Great Plains. These are just some of the popular stereotypes of Native Americans, and like most stereotypes they give a false impression.

This series on *Native American Culture* presents six books on various aspects of Native American life: child rearing, arts and crafts, daily life, tribal law, spiritual life, and the invasion by Europe. By reading these books, you will learn that there is no single Native American culture, but instead many different ones. Each Native American group or tribe in the past, as well as today, is a separate nation. While tribes may share some similarities, many are as different from one another as the English are from the Spanish.

The geographic focus of this series is the North American continent (United States and Canada), with special attention to the area within the present-day United States. However, Native Americans have lived, and continue to live, in Central America and South America. In addition, the authors of each book draw upon a wealth of historical information mainly from a time between the 1500s and 1900s, when most Native Americans were first contacted by European explorers, conquerors, and settlers. Much is known about this period of Native American life from documents and observations recorded by Europeans who came to North America.

It is also important to understand that Native Americans have a much longer and more complex history on the continent than just the past 500 years. Archaeologists have excavated ancient Native Americans sites as old as 12,000 years. The people who lived at these sites were among the first residents of North America. They did not keep written records of their lives, so the only information known about them comes from their stone tools and other remains that they left behind. We do know that during the thousands of years of Native American settlement across the continent the cultures of these early inhabitants changed in many important ways. Some of these cultures disappeared a long time ago, while others have survived and continue to change today. Indeed, there are more than 1.5 million Native Americans currently living in the United States, and the federal government recognizes over 500 tribes. Native Americans are in all walks of life, and many still practice traditions and speak the languages of their ancestors. About 250,000 Native Americans presently live on some 278 reservations in the country.

The books in this series capture the wonderful richness and variety of Native American life from different time periods. They remind us that the story of America begins with Native Americans. They also provide more accurate images of Native Americans, images that I hope will enable you to challenge the stereotypes.

Jordan E. Kerber, Ph.D.
Director of Native American Studies
Colgate University

Chapter

Native American Origins

When Christopher Columbus went ashore on the land that is now known as the Americas, he called the native peoples Indians. He thought that he had arrived in India. In reality, he had accidentally come upon a world that was unknown to his own.

This world and its peoples had existed for thousands of years. Native Americans were living in the Americas by the end of the Ice Age, about 12,000 years ago. It is thought that they migrated from Asia, which was connected to Alaska by a land bridge, when the water in the oceans was much lower than it is today.

Over thousands of years, these first peoples crossed the continents. As groups separated and moved on, they lost contact. A number of languages developed, and different groups, or tribes, formed their own beliefs, values, and behaviors. The tribes began to settle in certain areas. During all of these changes, their cultural ways of life developed. Legends were born, and laws were established.

Opposite:
A Native American boy in traditional dress for the Native American Festival in Hollywood, Florida, in January 1992. This four-day cultural festival brought together tribes from the United States and Canada.

Life, however, did not stay the same forever. As Native Americans continued to migrate, they came into contact with other tribes. New ways of life were learned, and cultures continued to change.

As a consequence, Native Americans living in specific areas of North America shared cultural traits with other Native Americans who lived near them. However, these groups were not exactly alike. Their histories were different in certain ways. They may have spoken very different languages or had different ways of governing themselves.

Non-Native Americans also greatly affected Native American cultures. During the 1500s and 1600s, the Spanish introduced horses, livestock, firearms, and disease to Native Americans living in the Southeast and Southwest regions of what is today the United States. As the French and English made their way across eastern North America during this same time, they began to trade for the Native Americans' fur pelts, which became very popular in Europe. In addition, Native Americans began to want the firearms, iron pots, steel knives, glass beads, and many other items that the Europeans had.

As Native Americans acquired horses and guns, their lives changed. Warfare increased, as tribes began to compete for furs in order to trade for European goods. Horses and guns also caused the Plains culture to thrive, because buffalo hunting became much easier.

When non-Native Americans started settling the land, Native American tribes were pushed out. Wars erupted between the native people and newcomers. Fighting did not end until the late nineteenth century.

By that time, most Native Americans were forced by the U.S. and Canadian governments to live on tracts of land known as reservations. They were governed by certain non-Native Americans, called agents, and were often cheated out

Many tribes lost their lands to Europeans and American settlers who sought open spaces to build new homes. In this painting, Native Americans on the plains watch as a train passes through what were once their lands.

of food and other goods. Children had to attend reservation schools, where they were forced to learn the non-Native Americans' ways of life. Native Americans were sometimes whipped if they spoke their native language.

Today, Native Americans live much like non-Native Americans. They own land, drive cars and trucks, live in modern houses, work in a wide variety of jobs, and fight the nation's wars. Many still live on reservations, however, and participate in tribal ceremonies, sing their peoples' songs and dance their dances, and tell the stories that have been handed down to them for generations. In these ways, many Native American traditions have been preserved.

In 1907, dressed in modern clothing, students and teachers pose for this picture at the U.S. government school on the Swinomish Reservation in La Conner, Washington.

Tribal traditions vary across the continent, but there are many similarities among tribes. In raising their children, for example, most Native American parents were not very harsh disciplinarians. Usually, they did not spank their children. In many Native American cultures, children received physical and moral training from their parents, grandparents, or other family members. Nearly all tribes performed ceremonies on certain important occasions, such as births, a boy's first kill on a hunt, the naming of children, and the passage from childhood to adulthood.

Although today's Native Americans cannot grow up in the same world that their ancestors did, they can be raised by their family in some traditional ways. Age-old ceremonies surrounding birth, adolescence, and marriage are still performed. Children play some of the same games that their tribespeople first played centuries ago, and parents still value the traditions they pass on to their children. The following chapters will explore the similarities and differences between the child rearing techniques and traditions of Native American tribes all over North America.

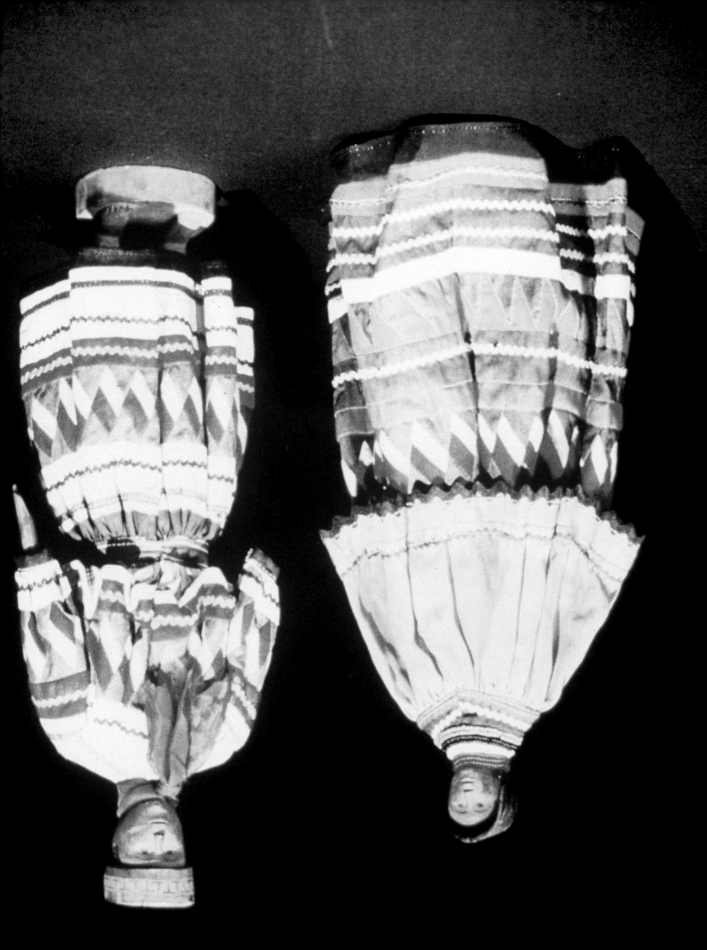

The East

In the eastern part of what is now the United States, a distinct group of Native American tribes hunted, gathered, fished, and farmed the land. These tribes lived as far north as the Saint Lawrence River (which runs along part of the U.S.-Canadian border) and the Great Lakes, all the way south to what is today Florida, and as far west as the Mississippi River. Although this area is quite large, the Native Americans who once lived there were in some ways very similar. They are described today as tribes of the Eastern Woodlands.

The Northeast

Opposite: Seminole children played with male and female dolls and dressed them in tribal clothes.

By the time Europeans came to the continent of North America, the Northeast was home to many tribes that lived in villages. Tribes were divided into clans, which were made up of many families. These Northeast tribes raised corn, squash, and beans. They fished, collected wild plants, and hunted wild game, such as deer, bear, and wildfowl. They

13

lived in dwellings made of bark and animal skins and wore clothes made from animal skins that were often decorated with porcupine quills or materials from other native animals.

One important tribal group of the East was the Iroquois. By 1570, five tribes that spoke Iroquoian—the Mohawks, Oneidas, Onondagas, Cayugas, and Senecas—had formed a political group called the Iroquois Confederacy, or the Iroquois League. Although their villages were widespread across what is today upstate New York, they were well united.

The foundation of Iroquois society was the fireside, which was composed of the mother and her children. Each fireside was part of a larger group, called the longhouse. Several longhouses constituted a clan, and the clans made up what the Iroquois called "a group of sisters and brothers." These groups made up the Iroquois nation.

The longhouse was also a long structure made of curved wooden poles covered with sheets of bark. Several Iroquois families lived in one longhouse. All authority stemmed from the chief matrons, or women who headed the longhouses. One of their most important duties was to keep track of the names owned by their clan. Names went back into the clan pool when people died, or when they gave them up. Names that were not being used could be given to newborn babies at the Green Corn Festival or Midwinter Festival.

The Iroquois had a number of names throughout their lives, but only one at a time. A name was thought to contain the thinking part of the soul. Having a certain name would cause a particular personality to develop. Some names were actually titles, and people who held important positions were usually given a series of names that led up to these title names. With each new name, an individual tried to behave as a person having that particular name should behave. This system of learning through naming may have been part of the Iroquois training for leadership.

Iroquois children were taken care of by their mothers. Babies were bound on cradle boards, a bed of animal skin attached to a wooden frame. Mothers carried these cradle boards on their backs. They took them to the fields and hung the cradle boards on the limbs of trees. The babies swung there, watching the world from an adult's height, while the women farmed.

When they were old enough to walk, Iroquois children went to the fields and helped their mothers. They also had small jobs to do around the longhouse and were allowed to participate in ceremonies.

Children were never spanked, but they were punished for misbehaving. Water was thrown in their faces, or, in extreme cases, they were frightened by a person called

In August 1925, members of the Narragansett, a Northeastern tribe, participated in a baby naming ceremony in front of the Old Indian Church in Charlestown, Rhode Island.

Longnose. This fictional character was a cannibal clown who chased bad children until they agreed to be good. A disobedient child was sent out of the longhouse at night, and a relative wearing the Longnose mask frightened the child into obedience.

At the age of eight or nine, boys and girls began to follow different paths. Iroquois boys formed groups and played at hunting and making war. Usually, their groups wandered about in the forest for days at a time. Girls stayed close to their mothers, learning to cook and sew.

When boys and girls reached adolescence, they usually went out into the forest to fast (go without food) for a few days. Sometimes they had a vision and acquired a guardian spirit. Then they went back to the village. At this time, boys began to hunt. They also participated in games like lacrosse with warriors from other villages. The games were rough, and players were often hurt.

When it was time to marry, the women in the family picked a partner for a boy or girl. There was no religious ceremony. The groom just moved directly into his bride's longhouse and adulthood began.

The Great Lakes

West of the Iroquois, in the Great Lakes region, were many tribes that spoke several different languages. The Ojibwa (also known as the Chippewa) and the Ottawa ranged the territory around the Great Lakes. Also living in this region, around the area that is now Green Bay, Wisconsin, was the Winnebago tribe. South of them were the Potawatomis, to whom the Ojibwa and Ottawa were said to be related. Other tribes were the Menominee, Sauk, Fox, Miami, and Kickapoo.

The Ojibwa, one of the largest tribes in North America, traveled with the seasons. They moved to hunting grounds

17

in winter, to maple groves in spring, then to berry patches, gardens, and fishing spots in summer, and on to rice fields in the fall. At each location, the women put up wigwams. These cone-shaped constructions were covered with birchbark and heated with a wood-burning fire.

The day after a child was born, the Ojibwa gave a feast. The people ate meat and smoked pipes. If twins were born, a special feast was given, because twins were considered to be sacred. A baby was usually named by an elder who had received the power of name-giving through a dream. If the child became sick, a new name was given.

Ojibwa cradle boards were made of cedar and covered with soft weasel or squirrel skins. With swamp moss used below the waistline as a diaper, babies were then wrapped tightly in soft, tanned deerskin and bound to the cradle boards.

The cradle board helped train the baby's back, so that later the child would have good posture. The Fox tribe believed that cradle boards helped prevent babies from having a long head, a hump-back, or bowed legs. Cradle boards also permitted mothers to carry their babies while traveling or working. Unlike the Iroquois, when taken to the fields, the Fox cradle boards did not hang from tree limbs. Instead, they were propped up against a tree.

An Ojibwa family stands outside their tipi. Both wigwams and tipis were used by the Ojibwa for shelter.

Young boys of the Great Lakes region, such as this child named "Pulls the Bow," were taught to hunt using the same weapons as their fathers.

If children were obedient, they were sometimes given rewards, such as maple sugar, a toy carved of wood, or a doll made of grass. Discipline was not harsh. Like the Iroquois, tribes in the Great Lakes region threw water at a child as a means of punishment. The Fox and Winnebago tribes preferred to make a little girl fast for a short time, so that she could think about her misbehavior.

Ojibwa children played making camp, hide-and-seek, and many other games. Adults played games as well. Like the Iroquois, they played lacrosse.

Elders taught children Ojibwa customs through stories, dances, songs, and chants. Grandmothers told legends to children from the ages of five to ten. These stories were amusing, historical, and often had a moral value. Through this instruction, the elders sought to increase children's understanding and wisdom.

After boys turned seven, they received instruction from older men on how to hunt and fish. Girls remained with their mothers and elders, from whom they learned how to make things for household use, such as the birchbark mats used to cover houses. They also learned how to take care of their homes and how to prepare hides so that they could become responsible adults.

In the last stage of childhood, an Ojibwa youth asked an elder for guidance. Parents selected marriage partners. There was no ceremony. A groom simply went to live with the family of his bride. After one year, a couple moved into their own wigwam.

The Southerners

The Shawnee, whose name means "southerners," lived in what is today Ohio, Pennsylvania, South Carolina, and Tennessee. They were the more southerly of the Eastern Woodlands tribes. They were closely related to Native Americans in the North, but they traveled widely and also came into contact with Native Americans in the Southeast.

Many Shawnee families hoped for sons more than daughters, but they treated children of both sexes with equal kindness. Shortly after a child was born, the parents would arrange a naming ceremony. A name placed the child in a clan.

Shawnee babies were bound on cradle boards to help their backs grow straight. A child's head was even more tightly bound to the board so that it would grow flat at the crown. This spot was where Shawnee men wore a silver hair plate and eagle feather.

Children were taught that good conduct brought reward and evil conduct brought sorrow. Unlike many Native American tribes, the Shawnee were harsh with their children when they misbehaved. They punished them by talking about their faults and scratching their thighs with a block of wood pierced with pins or hard thorns.

When a Shawnee boy was about nine years old, he would begin special training to learn endurance and self-control. In the fall, after the first frost, a father made his son run to a nearby creek and plunge into the cold water. Eventually, when a father felt his son was ready, the boy had to plunge in four times. This training for endurance continued among the Shawnee well into the twentieth century.

Older men and women, called grandpas and grandmas (whether or not they were related), helped instruct children. They gave advice and comfort. Grandmas taught girls about becoming women.

Boys and girls rarely played together. Boys wrestled, ran races, rode ponies, fished, and hunted. They made their own toys and played various ball games. Girls played at mimicking their mother's household tasks, making a variety of cakes, and molding pottery out of mud.

At the age of twelve or thirteen, boys were sent into the woods to fast and seek a spirit helper. A spirit helper was believed to appear in a vision in the form of an animal or bird. It gave a boy instructions and promised to aid him in future years.

When parents considered a child ready for marriage, they selected a mate. The groom's mother gave presents to the bride's mother. If the gifts were accepted, the bride's family prepared a great feast and took it to the young man's house. There they left the bride, and the feast began. Then the couple was considered married.

The Southeast

Tribes that lived south of the Shawnee spoke several different languages. The Cherokee, living in what is now North Carolina, South Carolina, and Tennessee, had the largest tribe in the Southeast. Their towns, organized under one principal chief, contained up to 200 dwellings.

Far west of this region, in what is now Arkansas, was the Quapaw tribe. In the southern part of the present-day state of Mississippi were the Biloxis, and in the central part, the Natchez. The Natchez lived in villages that were built around large earthen mounds. Here, the leading men of the tribe lived in wooden temples, and a powerful chief, similar to a king, was the supreme ruler.

In between, within the present-day states of Mississippi, Tennessee, and Alabama, were the Choctaw, Chickasaw, Creek, and many other tribes. These southeastern tribes believed that the younger of a set of twins was likely to become a diviner. Diviners could diagnose diseases and were highly respected. To strengthen their children, southeastern tribes used a ritual known as the water treatment. The Choctaw plunged infants into cold water, believing that it would keep them from death.

Among the Choctaw, Chickasaw, and Creek, there were typically two kind of names—names given to babies and names given to warriors. A child's name was usually one that described some aspect of character or appearance. Among the Chickasaw, these names were often of animals such as the fox.

Like tribes in the North, these southern cultures bound their children to cradle boards. They, too, believed the cradle board would help a child grow straight and strong. Most southeastern tribes also used the cradle boards to shape a child's skull. The Choctaw put boys in the cradle boards with their heads resting on a hole and a sandbag on their foreheads. The sandbags made their foreheads flat.

Children were never whipped, and boys were never disciplined by their mothers. If necessary, a mother took her son to an older man, usually her brother, for punishment. This man used the cold water treatment, throwing it all over the boy's body.

For strength and endurance purposes, children were made to plunge into cold water when they awakened. Like the Shawnee, some were eventually required to do this four times before being considered strong. Bathing was believed to increase one's chance of survival. The Natchez made a great noise when they jumped in the water, both to keep warm and to scare the alligators away.

One of the most important goals for a boy was to attain a war name, or title. Until then, he had to perform the tasks of a child. The war titles of the Creek were owned by the various clans. One name was usually of an animal and the other described the man in battle. For example, a warrior might be called Heartless Deer or Crazy Snake.

One account tells of other ways that names were given to warriors. In this incident, the Choctaw were attacked by their enemies, the Muscogee. The Choctaw beat them back and pursued them as they rode away. One young man, known as The Careless, rode far ahead of his companions and killed a Muscogee. As his companions approached, they noticed that a few Muscogee were turning back to attack The Careless. The Choctaw yelled out what would in English be "Quickly, run you." He did as they said, and was thereafter called Quickly Run You.

When it came time for marriage, a young man would tell his mother a woman's name. His mother would then talk to the mother of the young woman, and they would both go to the heads of the families to get consent. Then a ceremony would be arranged. The young man would go to the woman's village with his relatives and friends. On the day of the marriage, a "chase" was usually staged. The young woman would pretend to run away, and the man would chase her and bring her back. A feast would be held, and the couple would agree to be married. The man then lived in his wife's village, and their children belonged to her clan.

Opposite:
Choctaw women created beautiful baskets with regional grasses.

Chapter

3

The Great Plains

Reaching from the Mississippi River west to the Rocky Mountains, and from the Saskatchewan River in Canada south to central Texas, is a vast area known as the Great Plains. In its eastern part, are the tall grasses of the prairies. Westward, in what is called the high plains, rain falls less often and the grasses are short.

In the western plains, Native Americans hunted and gathered their food. In the east, where rainfall was more frequent, the people learned to farm. As agriculture became more important, villages became more permanent. These farmers did not have to roam in search of food. They did, however, continue to hunt.

By the time non-Native Americans had reached the plains in the sixteenth century, these two ways of life had already developed. Those who farmed and hunted lived in earthlodges, dome-shaped structures made from logs and covered with grass and mud. Those who lived in the dry,

A Sioux child, called John Lone Bull, poses for a photo.

western plains hunted buffalo and lived in tipis, cone-shaped tents constructed of poles and covered with buffalo hides.

Of the farmers, there were the Osage, Missouri, Kansa, Oto, Omaha, Iowa, Ponca, Arikara, Mandan, Hidatsa, Pawnee, Wichita, and a few other Dakota groups. Many of these tribes had clans similar to those of the tribes in the East. They sought visions from the supernatural in vision quests. They also had shamans, whom they thought could read the future, diagnose sickness, and perform magical acts.

The second cultural group was made up of the Blackfoot, Gros Ventre, Assiniboine, Crow, Sioux groups known as the Teton Dakota, Cheyenne, Arapaho, Comanche, Kiowa, and Kiowa-Apache. When non-Native Americans brought guns and horses to the continent, hunting the buffalo became easier and life on the plains flourished.

The Omaha

The Omaha lived along the Missouri River in what is today western Iowa and eastern Nebraska. In English, their name means "those going against the current." As one of the tribes of the eastern plains, they were villagers and farmers. They lived in earthlodges most of the year, but they also left their villages in search of buffalo.

Like other Plains Indians, the Omaha made war, especially against the Sioux. Like the western Plains Indians, they also had many tribal societies. The Bear Dreamers was a society that used tricks in their rituals, such as swallowing long sticks. Another group, called the Buffalo Society, took care of the sick.

Ceremonies played an important part in the lives of Plains Indians. After an Omaha child was born, a ritual was held and a prayer was recited. The baby was given a name and a pair of moccasins, or soft leather shoes. The moccasins had a hole in them so that if the Great Spirit called for the baby, the baby could say, "I can't travel now, my moccasins are worn out."

Omaha babies were carried about in cradle boards, and the boards also served as beds. If the mother was not traveling or working outside, she laid her baby on soft animal hides where the infant could kick and move about freely. When the baby was a little older and able to cling, the mother placed the baby inside her robe on her shoulder. The baby slept there close to his or her mother.

In some tribal societies, moccasins were given to newborns. An artist from the Lakota, a Plains tribe, crafted these colorful, beaded moccasins.

Sometimes when babies cried, special people were asked to come and comfort them. These people were thought to understand the sounds that babies made and could find out what babies needed.

When an Omaha child began to walk, a ceremony called Turning the Child was held. If the child was a boy, a lock of his hair was cut to bless him and to dedicate his life as a warrior for the protection of the tribe. After this ceremony, the training of a child began.

Children were taught to respect their elders, to obey their parents, and to be peaceable with one another. Much time was spent teaching children the Omaha language and the proper pronunciation of it. Girls were taught how to sit and how to rise. They also had to move about without being noisy. Boys could sit any way they wished, but as they became older, they had to learn how to sit steadily on their heels and rise quickly.

Children learned the history and traditions of their tribe during storytelling. On winter evenings, everyone sat about the fire and listened to the elders tell stories. The old story-tellers drew on their knowledge of the tribe's myths and fables, and on their memories of things that had happened. They told of the *gajazhe*, the little people who played about the woods and prairies leading people astray.

The Omaha enjoyed many different games. Boys played whip top in winter. They made tops out of wood and spun them on the ice. While sitting around the fire, they played a string game called cat's cradle, or the litter, by the Omaha. They also played a game with prairie grass. A bunch of grass was dropped on the ground. Each player tried to pull out pieces without disturbing the bunch, much like the game of pick up sticks.

Children made many of their toys with clay. They molded dishes, pipes, dolls, tents, and many other things that they were used to seeing in their world. Corncobs were sometimes used as dolls, and corn husks were used to make warbonnets.

Both boys and girls played games with balls. The girls played a game in which two balls were tied together with a stick. Two teams were formed, and goals were set up at either end of the playing field. Starting at the center, each side tried to prevent the other's balls from reaching the goal.

While still young, boys and girls played together. Girls played in their own miniature tipis. Sometimes the boys cut the tent poles for the girls, and a mother's robe was used as a tent cover. When it came time to follow the buffalo herds and pack up the camp, these play households were then also packed up.

A Piegan child stands in front of her miniature tipi. Plains children often "played house" in smaller versions of their homes.

Both boys and girls played at going on buffalo hunts. A boy was either a pretend hunter or pony. The play tent was packed, and the boy-pony pulled along the household bundle. The boy could play a good, peaceful animal or a high-kicking, disobedient one. Sometimes, boys carried their pony reputations throughout their lives. Old women would point to old playmates and laugh, saying, "He used to be a very bad pony."

By imitating their elders, both girls and boys learned about their roles as adults. Women had to prepare animal skins, make clothing, and cook. Men had to hunt and show themselves to be courageous.

This boy's beaded shirt was made by a Comanche woman. Women were always responsible for making the clothes for their families.

During adolescence, a girl was given a ceremony to welcome her to adulthood. Usually, one of the tribe's chiefs tattooed her with marks of honor. A round spot on her forehead represented the sun. After this tattoo was complete, a song was sung. Then other tattoos were added.

If a marriage was arranged for a young woman by her parents, her groom was usually an older man. He gave presents to her parents, and then she was delivered to his lodge on a pony led by four old men. If a young man and woman wanted to marry, they sometimes eloped. When they returned, the young man's father held a feast and gave gifts to the woman's parents.

The Arapaho

The Arapaho called themselves *Inuna-ina*, which in English means "our people." It is thought that they once lived in what is today Minnesota and North Dakota, but migrated to the headwaters of the Missouri River. At some point, they became like many other Plains Indians. They learned to ride horses, live in tipis, and follow the buffalo.

One Arapaho custom, which many other tribes also performed, was the Sun Dance. This ceremony, held once a year when berries were ripening, asked for the renewal of nature. Participants went without food and sleep for days, gazing at the sun and performing rituals. For use in ceremonies, the Arapaho made medicine bundles, which were containers that carried objects thought to have magical powers. The long tobacco pipe, or sacred pipe, was the most special of these objects. It was only smoked in ceremonies and on very special occasions.

War was a central part of Arapaho society. Young men were initiated into military societies, or clubs. Warriors participated in ceremonies before and after battles. They sang certain songs and performed special war dances.

Among the Arapaho, it was typical for fathers to teach their sons the ways of the tribe.

Many names belonging to the tribe originated in activities associated with war. A man always changed his name after killing or striking an enemy during warfare. Women, too, changed their names after performing an extraordinary deed. Newborns were named by an older man or woman, but no one kept the name given at birth. Even as children, Arapaho were given new names if they became sick.

Among the Arapaho, life began with a bath and the shaping of the head. Immediately after a child's birth, a woman shaped the child's head into a round ball. Then, the grandmother sat her grandchild on her knee and splashed the baby with cold water. A child was bathed in this way until he or she could walk. After the bath, the child was rubbed with a mixture of red earth and animal fat. Baby clothes were made of buffalo hide, and babies were placed in cradle boards.

In Arapaho culture, birth was not celebrated with a feast. However, a child did get his or her ears pierced in a ceremony. The piercing was usually performed by an old man who had been in many wars and who had pierced an enemy. Old women could perform the ceremony if they had pierced an enemy.

Fathers gave instructions to their sons, and mothers instructed their daughters. Other relatives, like grandparents, also helped out. When children misbehaved, parents did not discipline them. That job fell to one of the child's uncles. Either the water treatment was used, or a scary character, such as an owl or coyote, was chosen to frighten the child. When they behaved, children were usually rewarded with praise.

Boys and girls played with each other in the early years of childhood. Young girls had tipis about three feet high, set over buffalo hides on the ground. Along with the boys, they "played house" there. When they reached the age of

Arapaho girls learned tribal values and traditions from the women of the tribe.

nine or ten, however, boys and girls no longer spoke to each other unless it was necessary.

Often, two unrelated boys became good friends, lived in each other's houses, and eventually went to war together. Girls also had best friends. Often, for both the men and the women, these close friendships lasted throughout life.

At about the age of twelve, boys joined their first ceremonial lodge. From that time on, they usually associated only with members of their lodge. It became important at this time for them to start physical training. They swam and ran races. They walked long distances and carried heavy weights on their backs. They also wrestled, sometimes challenging boys of other tribes.

Girls also ran races and played, but play life usually ended at puberty. No feasts were given to welcome them to adulthood. At that point, they began learning how to cook, sew, and care for the home.

When it came time to marry, a young man approached the brother of the young woman he wished to wed. The brother then talked to his parents, and, if they approved, he talked to his sister. She could then refuse the young man or agree to marry him.

At a marriage ceremony, gifts were exchanged between the relatives of the bride and groom. A tipi was put up for the couple and furnished with reed beds, fur robes, and other household equipment. Following a feast, older men prayed for a newly married couple.

The Southwest

The American Southwest, considered mostly as the present-day states of Arizona and New Mexico, is very dry. Plants are sparse, but there are evergreen trees, piñon, juniper, and mesquite trees, as well as a variety of cactuses and shrubs. Animals are also scarce, but there are deer, rabbits, squirrels, mice, lizards, and large birds, such as eagles, hawks, and vultures.

In this vast area, the land is varied. There are flat-topped mesas separated by steep canyons, like the Grand Canyon, in the high country of the Colorado Plateau. There are also mountains, rivers, and desert lands.

Opposite:
These ruins in Canyon de Chelly, Arizona, were once home to the Navajo. The Navajo were forced from their canyon home and onto reservations when the U.S. government began to "civilize" Native Americans.

Two main ways of life evolved among the Native Americans living in this part of the country—farming and hunting. The Native Americans who farmed lived in permanent villages. Their dwellings, or pueblos, were made from brick or stone and had different apartment levels that were connected by ladders. The Pueblo peoples included the Hopi and Zuni tribes.

Some farmers lived in the desert lowlands or along the rivers. They made their homes in small huts covered with

Native Americans in the Southwest lived in many different types of homes. This hogan was a typical dwelling for the Navajo tribe.

earth or plants. These Native Americans included the Papago, Pima, Mojave, Yuma, Yaquis, and several other tribes.

The second way of life involved hunting and raiding the farmers. These raiders, like the Apache, lived in brush-covered houses called wickiups. Others, like the Navajo, lived in earth-covered houses called hogans.

The Hopi

The Hopi name is a shortened version of the name *Hopituh*, which means "peaceful ones." They lived near the Grand Canyon in what is today northern Arizona and grew corn, beans, squash, cotton, and tobacco. They also kept flocks of turkeys, because game was scarce.

In their desert homeland, the Hopi built their homes out of stones set in mud. The Hopi people had to travel far distances to find the pine and juniper trees that they used for making beams. After the building material was gathered and prepared, the women built the pueblos. Underground rooms, called kivas, were used by men as clubhouses and places of worship.

The tribe was organized into clans that were headed by shamans. The Hopi believed that guardian spirits, which were called kachinas, came down from the mountains each winter and lived inside the people's bodies until summer. Kachinas were believed to be good spirits, bringing forth melons and fresh corn at the beginning of each farming season.

During ceremonies, masked Hopi men impersonated the kachinas. In the Snake Dance, these men danced with live snakes around their necks and arms and inside their mouths. Scary kachinas, portrayed by masks with long teeth and bulging eyes, were called upon to frighten children who had misbehaved.

Children were told that these kachinas carried away bad girls and boys. At the parents' request, the leader of these kachinas, called *Soyoko*, appeared with her followers at the house where the children lived. The parents gave her food, pretending to defend their young ones against her. The children were thankful and tried to behave.

Children were also scolded and teased, and sometimes ridiculed, when they misbehaved. Another form of punishment was to pour cold water on children and then roll them in the snow. The Hopi encouraged their children to be friendly and to share with others. Children or adults who were considered cruel were usually shunned by others until they behaved. The Hopi people were focused on achieving peace in their lives.

Dressed as kachinas, Hopi men performed a kachina dance.

Hopi children were born into a society that had many rituals. Immediately after birth, a baby was rubbed with ashes so that his or her skin would always be smooth and warm. Then a child was bathed in suds made from warm water and pounded yucca root. After the bath, a baby was wrapped in a blanket and put into a cradle board made by the father's mother. To protect a baby's eyes, the house was darkened with blankets placed over the windows.

On the day of a naming ceremony, a child was bathed and given a name by the mother and sisters of the father. A child received many baths and names. At daybreak, a baby's mother and grandmother usually carried the child toward the rising sun. Prayers were said, and the child's names were repeated. An offering of cornmeal was sprinkled toward the sun. Then the family usually returned to the house to eat.

Children's play consisted of imitating adult activities. Girls played at making pottery, and boys played at rabbit hunting. Until about the age of six, boys could play freely, after that age, they had to help their fathers. In the morning, boys got up before sunrise and ran to a distant spring to bathe. Bathing was meant to make young boys strong and healthy.

The winter was the time to tell stories. It was believed that a person telling stories at any other time would be bitten by a snake or suffer other consequences. The stories were meant for children because they taught them Hopi traditions and morals, but both children and adults enjoyed the tales. The characters were usually animals—bears, rabbits, birds, and coyotes—that acted like humans.

At an early age, Hopi children learned about the ways and beliefs of their tribe. When only a few months old, they were taken to ceremonies. When children were old enough to ask questions, they received explanations.

Boys aged six to ten learned more about the kachinas at their initiations. These ceremonies often included whippings. Afterward, boys were allowed to participate in public dances.

A second initiation for boys occurred when they were about fifteen or sixteen. After this secret ceremony, boys belonged to either the Warrior Society, the Horn Society, the Singer Society, or the *Wuwucim* Society. They could not belong to more than one. Once the initiation was over, they were considered adults.

There were women's societies, too, but they were not the same as the men's societies. Girls did not undergo initiations, although there was a ceremony to welcome them into womanhood. They took part in a long grinding ceremony in which they ground corn for five days straight. On the fifth day, girls changed their hairstyle to that of the mature Hopi woman. Afterward, they were considered ready for marriage.

When a young woman wished to marry, she proposed to a young man. The union had to be approved of by their parents. Then, the young woman went to stay for several days with her groom's mother. During that time, she ground corn and the groom's aunts came around and staged a mud fight. The mock battle was always in good fun and was meant to show the young woman that her new aunts approved of her.

Finally, in the early morning of the last day of her stay, the young woman's family went to the groom's house. Her female relatives washed her hair and the groom's hair, twisting it together into one strand, a symbol of their being united for life. When their hair was dry, the couple went to the edge of the mesa to pray to the rising sun.

The Apache

Feared by many other tribes in the Southwest, the warlike Apache tribe really earned its name. The name *Apachu*, given to the tribe by the Zuni, means "enemy." For much of their history, the Apache raided more peaceful tribes for food and other goods.

Opposite:
This traditional Hopi hairstyle, called a squash blossom, was the symbol of a mature woman.

The numerous groups of Apache roamed far and wide, in areas that are now part of Arizona, New Mexico, Texas, Colorado, Oklahoma, Kansas, and Mexico. Among these different Apache bands were the Chiricahua, Mescalero, Jicarilla, Kiowa-Apache, and many others.

✳

44

Although the Apache were raiders, they also hunted and gathered food. When they could not get enough food in their rugged, desert homeland, however, they raided the Pueblo peoples. They also adopted ways of life from other Native American tribes. The western Apache took up farming, imitating the Pueblo. The Jicarilla became more like the Plains Indians, riding on horses in pursuit of buffalo and living in tipis.

There were many supernatural beings in Apache religion. *Ussen*, the Giver of Life, was the most powerful. Mountain Spirits, or *Gans*, were important in many ceremonies. Apache men dressed up in costumes and impersonated *Gans* in dances. They wore black masks, skirts, tall wooden headdresses, and body paint.

Among the Apache, children were so greatly prized that their place of birth became holy. Almost immediately after birth, a ceremony began. The baby was given a bath in lukewarm water and rubbed with a mixture of red ocher (a clay mixture) and grease. Then, the infant was wrapped in a blanket. Usually, this ritual involved sprinkling pollen or ashes, first in four directions and then on the child. For the Apache, the birth of twins was greatly dreaded. It was taken as a bad sign, and only one of two twins was expected to live to adulthood.

Names were given to Apache infants right away, but this first name was rarely kept through adulthood. As with many other tribes, cradle boards were used to hold babies. These boards were specially constructed by people who had earned the right to make them. Within the first month of life, babies had their ears pierced. This practice was believed to keep a child on the right path. Otherwise, a child would grow up wild and bad.

Until about the age of five or six, boys and girls played together. They listened to stories that taught them how to

45

Apache men listen as a story is told. Tribal storytelling helped boys learn how to act as men.

behave. One frequent character was Coyote, who showed them how *not* to act. He always did the wicked and silly things that bad people do.

Children also received training in manners. They learned not to run around a camp that was not their own. Boys were never to fight with girls. Children were not to ask for more food than they could eat. More than anything, children were not to make fun of the elderly.

If children misbehaved, they were ridiculed. If they cried too much, cold water was thrown on them. "Bogeys" were also called upon to scare disobedient children. The clown, who accompanied the *Gan* impersonators, was said to punish bad children by taking them away in a basket.

As part of their physical training and mental discipline, children were made to bathe in cold mountain streams. As

A young Apache girl participates in the puberty rites of her tribe. This ritual is one of the most sacred.

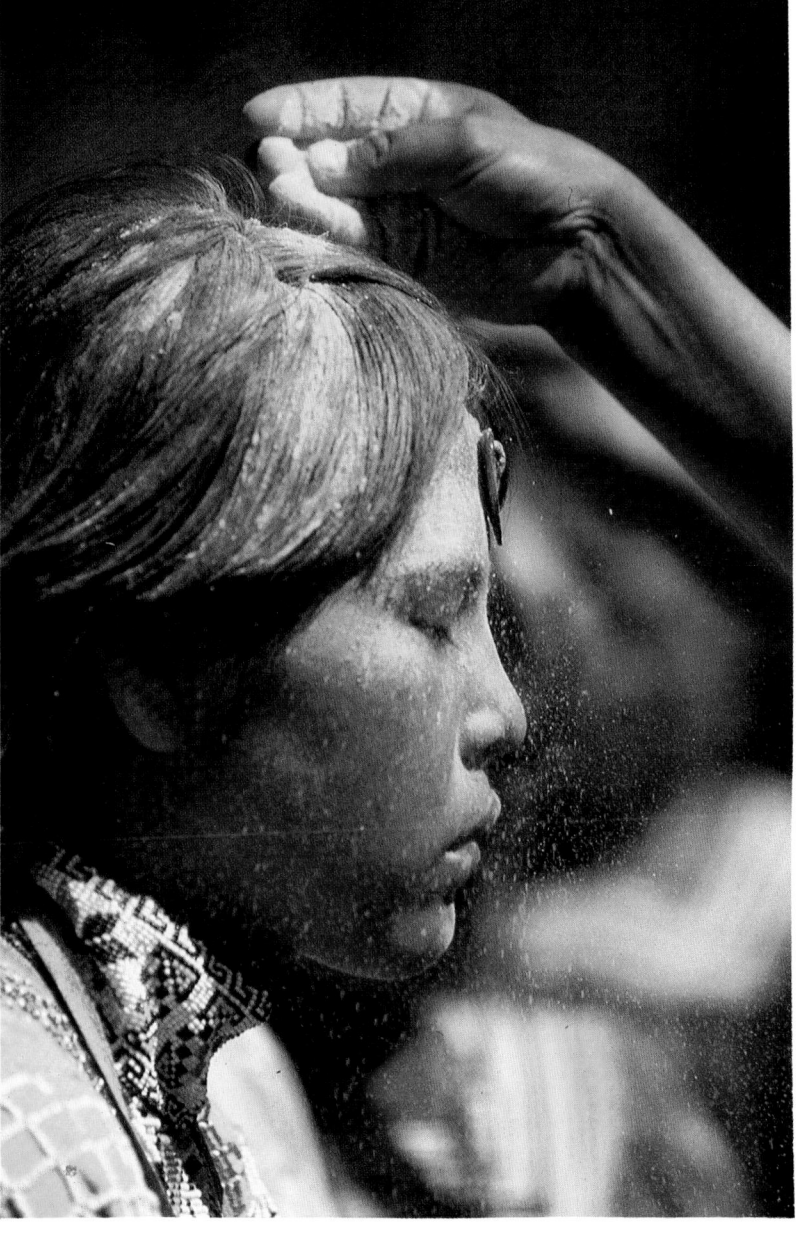

Toward the end of the Apache puberty ceremony, pollen, a symbol of fertility, is sprinkled over the girl.

boys grew older, they began to play at hunting and raiding. They worked with bows and arrows until their aim was accurate. When the men thought a boy was ready, they took him on a raid.

Adolescent girls were given a great celebration when they entered adulthood. The ceremony lasted for four days, with much singing and dancing. Through this puberty ceremony, young women were expected to learn how to achieve the four Apache objectives in life: physical strength, a good disposition, prosperity, and a healthy old age.

When a young man and woman wished to be married, their families began negotiating. The young man's family sent presents to the young woman. These gifts usually included horses, a saddle, a bridle, a gun, a blanket, and buckskins. Then, three older female relatives took the young woman to the man's camp. The couple was then considered married.

Chapter

The West

Beyond the Great Plains and the American Southwest, reaching westward to the Pacific Ocean and northward to Canada, are many varied regions. Some places are hot and dry. Others are wet and cool. Within this large area, which includes the present-day states of Colorado, Utah, Nevada, California, Oregon, Washington, Montana, and Idaho, are many different Native American tribes.

The Great Basin

In the rocky deserts and large salt flats of the Great Basin, where Death Valley and the states of Nevada and Utah are today, it was very difficult for Native Americans to live off the land. Usually, the people lived in wickiups and wore little clothing. There were few places to get water, so farming was impossible.

Depending on how far north or south they roamed, the tribes of the Great Basin collected roots, seeds, berries, and nuts. They hunted deer, antelope, and mountain sheep and

Opposite:
A Shoshone child, bundled on a cradle board on the Wind River Reservation in Wyoming.

49

roasted grasshoppers, lizards, mice, birds, rabbits, and prairie dogs. In what is now southern Idaho, these tribes also fished for salmon in the Snake River.

Because the tribes of the Great Basin moved around so much, families were not generally organized into big groups. Sometimes in the winter, many families would come together, but there were no clans and no real leaders. The wise members, known as talkers, gave advice. When groups did come together, Native Americans of the Great Basin danced, sang, gambled, and told stories. A place known as a sweathouse served as a men's club, a meeting-house, and lodging for unmarried men. Here, men also purified themselves with heat.

Of the tribes that lived in the Great Basin, such as the Ute, Shoshone, Bannock, and Paiute, some acquired horses and began to roam out to the plains. Some groups of Shoshone were great buffalo hunters by the time non-Native Americans came to the area.

Among the Shoshone, children were important members of the tribe. They were great helpers when it came time for gathering food. Their little fingers could easily separate small seeds, pluck berries, and dig carrots and potatoes.

As with many other Native American tribes, bathing after a baby's birth was a great ritual. A baby was bathed immediately after being born. The mother bathed every five days and the father took a bath every morning to stay strong. He usually left a present by the stream as an offer-ing, so that his child would stay healthy.

Children did not generally receive a name until they could talk. They were punished by being laughed at when they disobeyed or they were told scary stories about mean beasts that killed and ate noisy children.

As boys grew up, they were trained to hunt. They were not considered men until they had made their first kill. The meat from this first hunt was given to another family, and the boy was prayed over and given a bath on the following day.

Young girls learned to gather food and build fires. When they reached puberty, they were taught all the things they needed to know to become a wife. Usually, a girl's parents had chosen a husband for her while she was still a baby. When she married, gifts were exchanged between her parents and the parents of her husband. Then, she and her husband began to live together.

The Plateau

North of the Great Basin, situated between the Cascade Mountains to the west and the Rocky Mountains to the east, is an area called the Plateau. The mountains receive a great deal of rain and snowfall, and some of the tallest trees in the world grow there.

Between the mountains, in the Plateau, the land is fairly flat and gets very little rain. Although there was very little game to hunt on the flatlands, the fishing was good. Salmon were especially plentiful.

Living near the Snake and Salmon rivers, was the Nez Perce tribe. Their name, which means "pierced noses" in French, was given to them by the French. The Nez Perce called themselves *Nimipu*, meaning "the people." Some of them did wear nose pendants, but not all of them.

Before the early eighteenth century, when they acquired horses and learned to hunt buffalo, the Nez Perce lived like other Plateau tribes. They fished for salmon and hunted elk, deer, mountain sheep, and rabbit. They also gathered wild plants. The Nez Perce lived in brush-covered huts in the summer and earth-covered houses in the winter. They had a loose social structure, with no clans, powerful chiefs, or secret societies. This tribe did have shamans, however, and youths sought guardian spirits through vision quests.

When a baby was born, feasts were held for both the mother and child. Relatives gave them gifts. Babies were placed in cradle boards, where they stayed until they learned how to walk. Children were given names of important family ancestors because it was believed that such names would influence their development. Names could be changed at any time, though, especially if an individual accomplished something significant. In adolescence, when a young person came back from a vision quest, a formal naming ceremony was held. Names reflected guardian spirits, as well as outstanding personal characteristics, and they were regarded as private or family property. Therefore, nicknames were often used, and real names were rarely spoken.

Because grandparents cared for children, close ties developed between them. Children were often formal with their parents, but joked and teased with their grandparents, whom they respected very much. Children learned a lot from hearing their grandparents tell them about the tribe's legends and folklore. Grandfathers often instructed boys in

In 1970, clothed in traditional dress, a Nez Perce boy and girl participate in powwow dancing near Spalding, Idaho.

In 1891, as members of the first missionary society, Nez Perce children and adults pose for a picture in Spalding, Idaho.

fishing, riding horseback, hunting, and taking sweat baths. As part of their training, children were wakened early in the morning and were made to run to the bathing area, where uncles and aunts supervised them.

Infants were rarely disciplined. As they got older, though, they were whipped by special whippers. When one member of a group of children misbehaved or disobeyed, the whole group was punished.

To learn their people's ways of life, children began to work with parents at about age three. They were tied in the saddle and taken on horseback to the various hunting, fishing, root-digging, and berry-picking areas. They helped with toy bows and arrows and other special implements designed just for them.

By age six, children were contributing to the family's upkeep. Special ceremonies were held at this time for a boy's first game kill and a girl's first root digging and berry picking. Also at this time, another important event took place. An outstanding elder gave a private lecture to a child, reminding him or her of the tribe's morals.

Around the time of adolescence, both boys and girls were sent on quests to seek visions from guardian spirits. It was believed that children would grow up to be successful if they had a vision. Many youths had to go on several quests before having a vision.

At puberty, girls were given an elaborate ceremony. They were isolated with other girls in a special house, where an older female supervised them. They were urged to keep busy and think good thoughts, for it was believed that anything they did during this period would affect the rest of their lives. After about a week, the girls came back into the community as young women ready for marriage. Friends and relatives gave them gifts and new clothes. To show their new status as adults, they adopted a new hairstyle.

Marriage was a serious matter arranged by one head from each of two families in similar social position. Sharp differences in wealth and social status separated Nez Perce families into three classes. At the top, were families of powerful leaders. Most people were in the middle, and they could marry members of the upper class. Slaves captured in war were the lowest.

Female relatives negotiated marriage for a young man. If both families agreed to the union, the young man and woman visited each other and feasts were given. Mothers of the bride and groom made plans for the wedding. After a big feast, gifts were exchanged between the two families. Relatives of the groom gave horses, hunting and fishing implements, and buckskins. Those of the bride gave root bags, baskets, beads, and beaded bags. Afterward, the couple was considered husband and wife.

California and the Pacific Northwest

Over a long period of time, many different groups of Native Americans traveled over mountains and through deserts to the warm valleys, rivers, and coastal plains of what is now California. Native Americans have been living in this area for at least 10,000 years. Before non-Native Americans arrived, this area was home to a variety of Native American groups. Some were similar to tribes in other nearby areas— in the Southwest, Great Basin, or Pacific Northwest.

From northern California to southern Alaska lies an area about 150 miles wide. This is called the Pacific Northwest. There are many islands, forests, and streams. The Native Americans in this area lived on the coast, traveling and fishing by boat.

These Northwest tribes were skilled woodworkers. They built their rectangular houses from wood, which was usually cedar that was taken right from the forest. Outside, they put up totem poles, which were tall wooden logs that had beautiful and intricate carved faces. Shamans and members of secret societies could interpret their meanings.

Social status was determined by an individual's wealth. In a Pacific Northwest custom called the potlatch, families held feasts and gave away as many possessions as possible to prove how wealthy they were.

Living in the northernmost tip of what is now California, the Yurok were very much like other California tribes. They hunted and gathered their food and lived in villages in the winter. Like Native Americans in the northern part of California, they practiced the World Renewal Ceremonies, which were believed to renew the earth and promote the well-being of the tribe.

The Yurok were similar to other tribes of the Pacific Northwest. They fished for salmon in the Klamath River and built rectangular houses out of cedar. The Yurok also

A carved rattle of the
Haida, a tribe of the
Pacific Northwest.

determined social status by wealth. Their language was
similar to that of Native Americans living in the Northeast,
Great Lakes, and Southeast. However, in one way the
Yurok were like no other Native American tribe. They did
not consider land to be a source of life shared by the tribe.
Like non-Native Americans, the Yurok believed in ownership of the land. They measured wealth by land ownership
and sold land to one another.

The Yurok began life with much physical attention.
Babies were given a steambath of wild ginger, and for the
first ten days after birth, they were given a kind of nut soup
from a tiny shell. After twenty days, their grandmothers
began to massage their legs, to encourage them to start to
crawl about.

Children's first meals were salmon and deer meat.
When they were old enough to understand language, they
were told to eat slowly and not to take food without asking.
Mothers taught daughters, and fathers taught sons.

Fables also instructed children in good behavior. To
encourage children to eat slowly, they heard a story about a

buzzard who could not wait for his food. He tried to eat
the soup before it was cool enough. One day, he was so
hungry that he stuck his whole head in and scalded his
crown. Now, according to the fable, he does not touch
warm food anymore. He waits until his food is so old that it
stinks. Another fable described a rock that was said to have
once been a child who did not mind his parents. An owl
had taken hold of him and carried him to the rock, where he
sat and cried forever.

In their play, Yurok children built little houses. Girls
made dolls out of mud and put them into cradles. Boys
played with bows and arrows and toy canoes. For safety,
children were not allowed to play near the ocean or rivers.

Certain people among the Yurok were chosen to teach
children. The children were later tested by their grandfathers.
If they misbehaved during their lessons, it was thought that
they had seen bad spirits. These children were sent home,
and sometimes a shaman was called to treat them.

Boys became members of sweathouses as they grew. As
an adult, a man married by paying for a wife and taking her
to live in his house. Even after marriage, however, men
usually continued to live in sweathouses with other men,
instead of at home with their wives.

It is evident that Native Americans were not all alike in
the way they raised their children, but there were similarities. From birth to adulthood, ceremonies announced
different stages and passages, but the ceremonies differed
from one tribe to another. All children were allowed time to
play, but they also had to learn, work, and train their bodies.
Misbehaving children were ridiculed, punished, or frightened into obedience. Each tribe had its own way of living
and passed its beliefs and values on to its children. Among
the Native Americans today, whether in cities or on reservations, many of these traditional ways continue.

Glossary

clan A social group within a tribe that is made up of several families who are descended from a common ancestor.

cradle board A carrier for babies, made of wood, leather, animal hides, and other natural materials.

culture A specific set of beliefs, values, and behaviors shared by a group of people who usually have a common history.

earthlodge A large house made from logs and covered with branches and mud; usually dome-shaped.

fast To go without eating.

hogan A house built with logs and sticks and covered with mud or sod; usually cone-shaped. The Navajo tribe lived in hogans.

kachina One of hundreds of supernatural beings that many Pueblo believe live in the American Southwest. Wooden dolls of the kachinas are given to Pueblo children to teach them about these important spirits.

kiva An underground chamber where men in Southwest tribes gather to conduct religious ceremonies and boys learn tribal traditions.

longhouse A societal group among the Iroquois tribe; also, a dwelling in which several Iroquois families lived.

military society A club of warriors that is found among Plains Indians, whose members shared rituals and wore similar clothing.

potlatch A ceremony held by the Tlingit, Kwakiutl, and other Northwest Coast tribes. At a potlatch, the hosts offered their relatives and friends costly food and gifts to display their wealth and their power within their village.

powwow A conference or gathering of Native Americans; often characterized by feasts, dancing, and celebration.

pueblo Native American village made of large clay-brick dwellings. The many Southwest tribes that have lived in these types of houses, such as the Hopi and the Zuni, are known as the Pueblo.

reservation A tract of land set aside by the United States for a group of Native Americans. Usually, reservations were small plots of poor-quality land offered to Native Americans only after white settlers had seized their lands.

sachem A peace chief who was responsible for handling village affairs. Sachem also refers to a ruler or chief of allied tribes.

shaman A religious leader who cures illnesses and makes contact with the spirit world. Shamans are also known as medicine men.

sweathouse A place where men of the Great Basin tribes purified themselves with heat. Some were also used as clubhouses.

tipi A cone-shaped portable house made from a large animal-hide cover and a frame of wooden poles. Plains Indians decorated their tipis with paint.

totem pole A tall pole carved by Pacific Northwest tribes with symbolic faces whose meanings were interpreted by shamans and members of secret societies.

tribe A group of Native American people who share the same religious, cultural, and social beliefs.

vision quest The seeking of visions or dreams by depriving oneself of food and sleep. The vision quest was a rite of passage from childhood to adulthood.

wickiup A dwelling constructed with poles and covered with brush, grass, or reeds. The Apache lived in wickiups. Plains Indians also used wickiups as sweathouses.

wigwam A dwelling constructed with poles and covered with bark, animal skin, or woven mats. Tribes of the Northeast and Great Lakes used wigwams.

Further Reading

Andrews, Elaine. *Indians of the Plains.* New York: Facts On
  File, 1991.

Chandonnet, Ann. *Chief Stephen's Parky: One Year in the
  Life of an Athapascan Girl.* Billings, MT: Council for
  Indian Education, 1989.

Fulkerson, Chuck. *The Shawnee.* Vero Beach, FL: Rourke,
  1992.

Grant, Bruce. *Concise Encyclopedia of the American Indian.*
  Avenal, NJ: Outlet Book, 1989.

Hahn, Elizabeth. *The Pawnee.* Vero Beach, FL: Rourke, 1992.

Hirschfelder, Arlene. *Happily May I Walk: American Indians & Alaska Natives Today.* New York: Macmillan
  Publishing, 1986.

McCall, Barbara. *The Cherokee.* Vero Beach, FL: Rourke,
  1989.

_____. *The Iroquois.* Vero Beach, FL: 1989.

Mike, Jan. *Chana, An Anasazi Girl: Historical Paperdoll
  Books to Read, Color & Cut.* Tucson, AZ: Treasure
  Chest, 1991.

Sherrow, Victoria. *Indians of the Plateau & Great Basin.*
  New York: Facts On File, 1991.

_____ *The Hopis: Pueblo People of the Southwest.*
  Brookfield, CT: The Millbrook Press, 1993.

Stan, Susan. *The Navajo.* Vero Beach, FL: Rourke, 1989.

_____. *The Ojibwe.* Vero Beach, FL: Rourke, 1989.

Warren, Scott S. *Cities in the Sand: The Ancient Civilizations
  of the Southwest.* San Francisco, CA: Chronicle Books,
  1991.

Wood, Ted & Wanbli Numpa Afraid of Hawk. *A Boy Be-
  comes a Man at Wounded Knee.* New York: Walker &
  Co., 1992.

Index

Photo credits

Cover : ©Guy Monthan; p. 6: ©Philippe Brylak/Liaison USA;
pp. 9, 10–11, 17, 18, 26, 30, 42, 45: Library of Congress; pp.
13, 22, 31, 40:©Blackbirch Press, Inc.; p. 15: Courtesy of the
Rhode Island Historical Society; p. 25: ©Renato Rotolo/
Gamma-Liaison; p. 28: ©Gary Retherford/Photo Researchers,
Inc.; pp. 33, 35: Western History Collections, University of
Oklahoma Library; p. 36: ©Peter C. Jones/Liaison Interna-
tional; p. 38: ©North Wind Pictures; p. 46: ©Bill Gillette/
Gamma Liaison; p. 47: Cooper/Gamma Liaison; p. 48: ©Victor
Englebert/Photo Researchers, Inc.; pp. 52, 53: National Park
Service/Nez Perce National Historical Park; p. 56: ©Kjell B.
Sandved/Photo Researchers, Inc.